Philippe GAUBERT
The Essential Library, Bk. 1

for Flute and Piano

Edited, arranged and performed by
Sir James Galway

PIANO

Editor's Notes

Fantaisie, written in 1912, is dedicated to Leopold Lafleurance, who at the time was solo flutist in the Paris Opera. The beginning, *moderato quasi fantasia* allows you to shine with its free style. The *Assez lent*, is the middle section of the piece and should be played according to the tempo markings suggested by the composer. At bar 41 there is a cadenza leading to the conclusion of part one of the piece. The second part of the *Fantasie* gives you the opportunity to show off your finger technique and triple tonguing. I would recommend you practice your trills, which will add a nice touch of brilliance to the piece.

Nocturne and Allegro Scherzando was commissioned as a required concours piece for students at the Paris Conservatory in 1906 and dedicated to Philippe Gaubert's teacher and mentor, Paul Taffanel. It is indeed a real test piece for any flutist. The *Nocturne* is an opportunity for you to show off your best tone colors and intonation. The *Allegro Scherzando* is a great test for your fingers and gives you some idea of the standard of the flute class in the Paris Conservatoire. In the middle of all the fireworks, the piece returns to the beginning theme, but in the second octave. It finishes with some very difficult scales, arpeggios, double tonguing and octaves.

Madrigal is one of Gaubert's most performed works. It is considered a great introduction to Gaubert's style. The work begins in the lower register and returns there throughout the piece. Underlying the seemingly simplistic melody is the need for perfect synchronization of the flutist and pianist to execute the parallel harmonies in the piece.

The *Third Sonata* was composed in 1933 for Jean Boulze, solo flutist of the *Opéra et des Concerts Lamoureux*. In the first movement, *Allegretto*, I would recommend that you play with a tempo a little on the quick side. The reason for this is that it helps enormously with the breathing. A light touch upon the keys also helps toward the success of this piece. The key to the second movement also lies in the tempo, *Tres Moderé*. Do not be tempted into playing too slowly but try at all times to play with your most beautiful tone, again using a light touch upon the keys. The third movement should not be too slow in spite of the *Joyeux - Allegretto* tempo suggestion from Gaubert. The sonata is a wonderful piece and is a great opener for any recital.

Breathing and Posture

- Breathing is one of the most important and neglected elements in the quest for a good tone.
- Without a good breath control your chances of having the tone of your dreams will remain a dream.
- In order to obtain a beautiful tone you need to begin with your posture.
- Good posture is essential for good breathing. Without a good posture you cannot attain good breathing.
- I was fortunate as a teenager to learn the flute with a singer. She taught me to have a good posture and with it good breathing. They go hand in hand.
- There are plenty of singing demonstrations on the Internet connected with breathing and posture and I would urge you to look there for help.
- Nearly every book on singing contains a lot of material about posture and breathing. I suggest you look at something like *Singing for Dummies* as a good place to start.
- In my editions for Southern Music I have put in many breath marks, sometimes more than you might think necessary. I don't want to be short of breath at the conclusion of a phrase. One should have enough breath to support the tone at all times. Good breath control is the secret of a great tone.

The breath marks are of two kinds: (√) being a very quick and short breath whereas (') is a regular breath mark. For a short breath, I would recommend that you don't open your mouth so much but that you acquire the technique of taking a lot of breath through your lips in the embouchure position.

Sir James Galway

à L. Lafleurance

Fantaisie

for Flute and Piano

Philippe Gaubert

edited, arranged and performed by
Sir James Galway

Piano

Flute

Moderato, quasi fantasia *rit.* *a tempo*

Piano

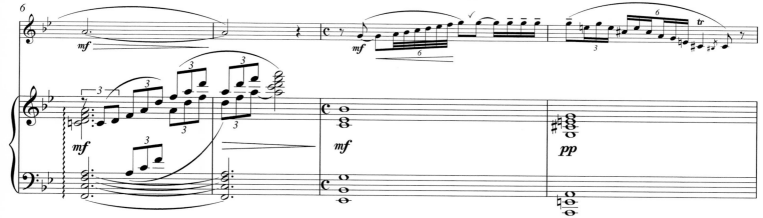

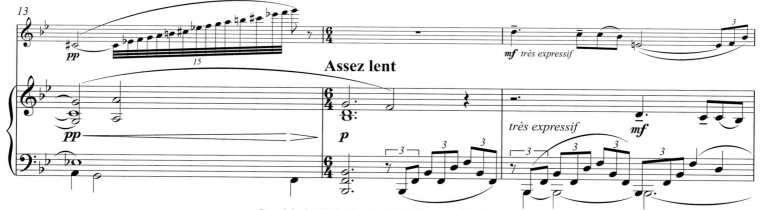

Assez lent

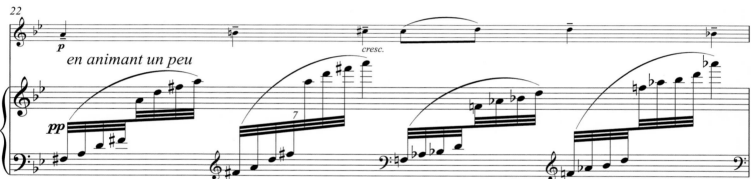

6

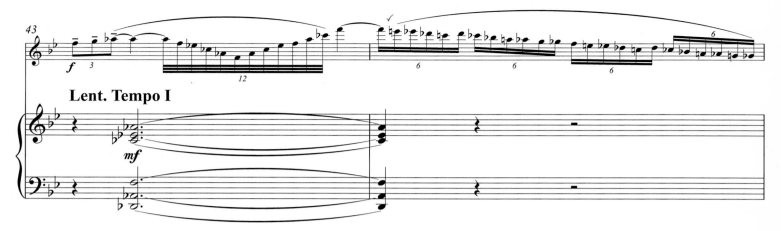

Lent. Tempo I

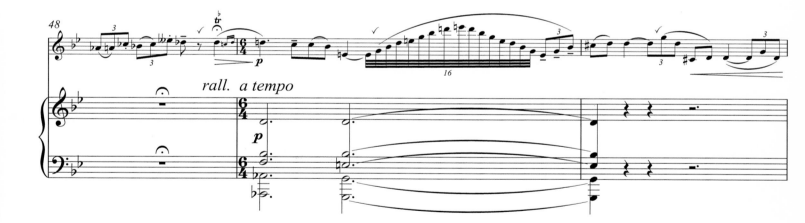

Vif (à un temps)

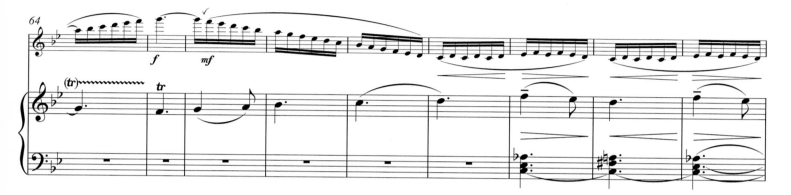

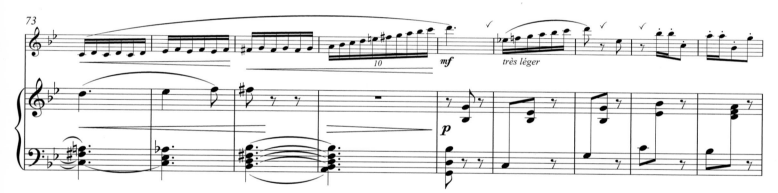

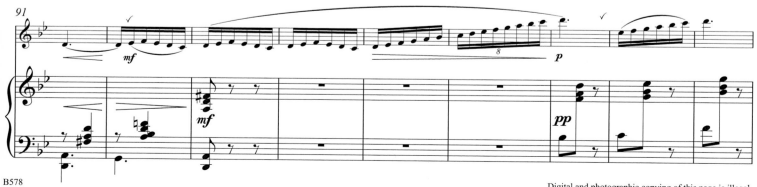

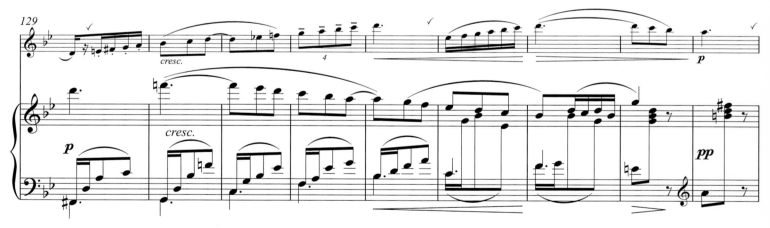

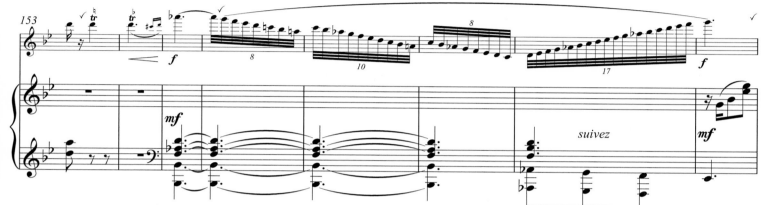

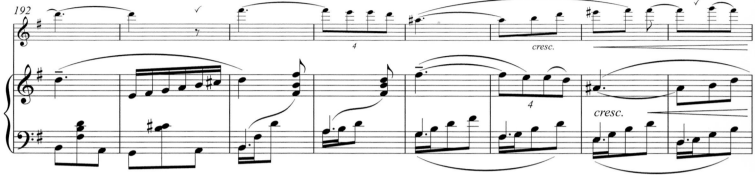

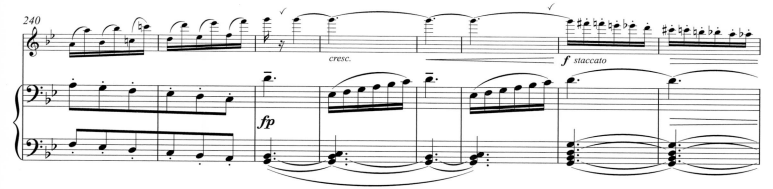

à mon cher Maître Paul Taffanel, Professeur au Conservatoire

Nocturne and Allegro Scherzando
Nocturne

Piano

Philippe Gaubert
edited, arranged and performed by
Sir James Galway

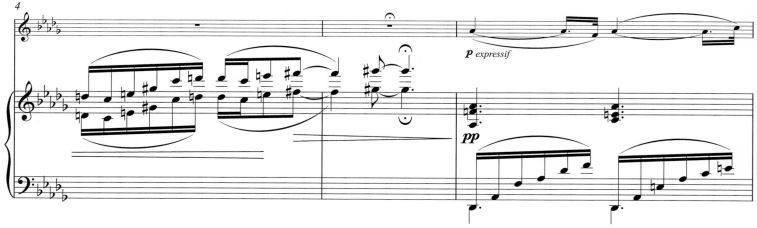

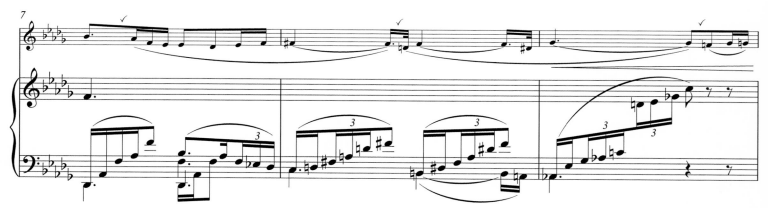

Allegro Scherzando

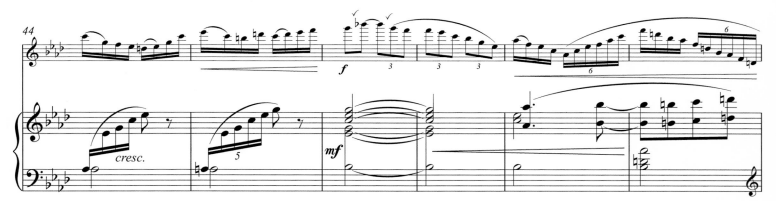

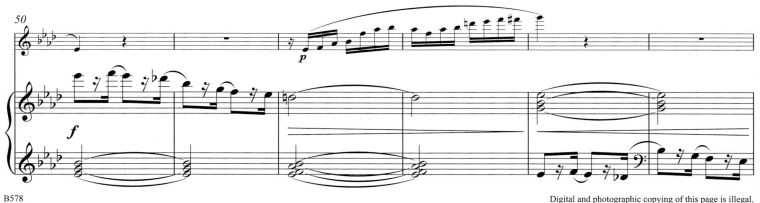

Un peu moins vite

a tempo

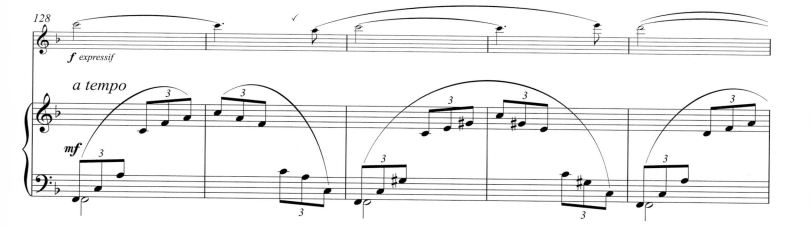

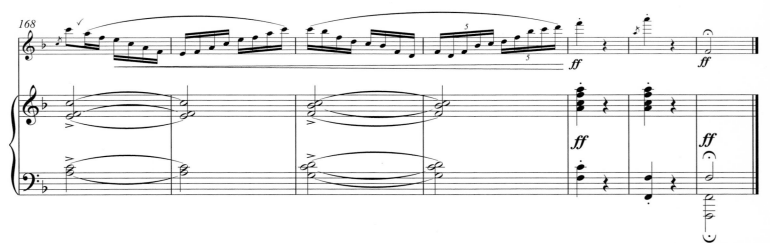

à Docteur Bucquoy
de l'Académie de Medecine

Madrigal

Philippe Gaubert
edited, arranged and performed by
Sir James Galway

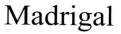

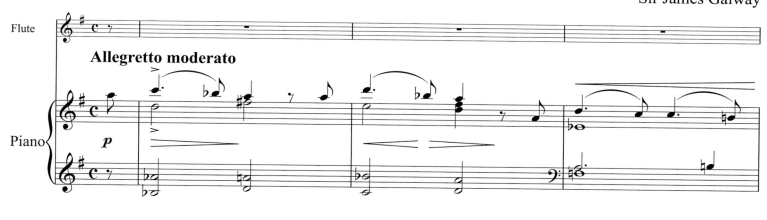

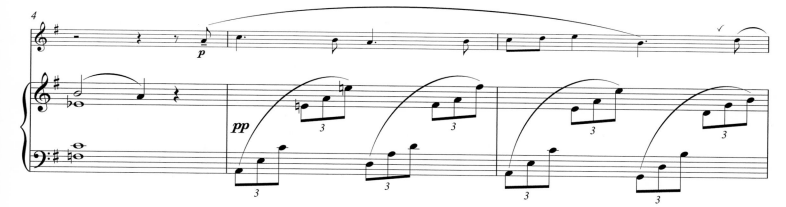

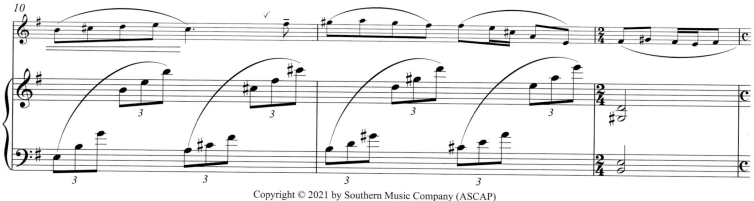

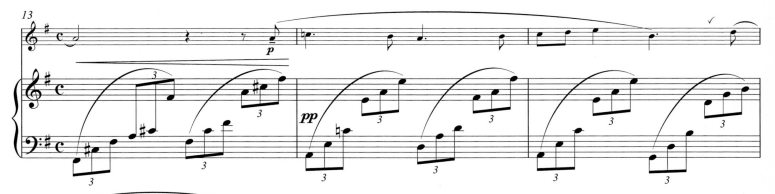

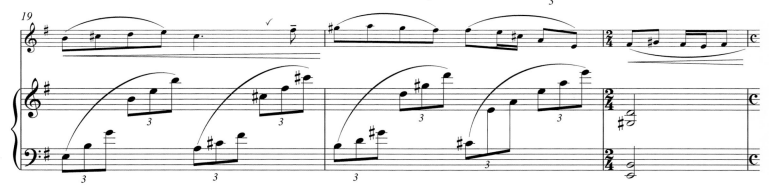

Philippe GAUBERT
The Essential Library, Bk. 1

for Flute and Piano

Edited, arranged and performed by
Sir James Galway

FLUTE

About the Editor

The living legend of the flute, Sir James Galway is regarded as the supreme interpreter of the classical flute repertoire. Through his extensive touring, over 30 million albums sold, Sir James has endeared himself to millions worldwide. Belfast born, Sir James studied in London and Paris before embarking on his prestigious orchestral career with Sadlers Wells and Royal Covent Garden, the BBC, Royal Philharmonic and London Symphony Orchestra, and then solo flautist with the Berlin Philharmonic under Herbert von Karajan.

Since launching his successful career as a soloist in 1975, he has performed with the world's leading orchestras and most prestigious conductors and has shared the stage with an amazing array of entertainers. Alongside his busy performing schedule, he makes time to share his wisdom and experience with the young through the Galway Flute Academy; encompassing his educational programs and online flute series, First Flute.

Among the many honors and awards for his musical achievements are the Recording Academy's President's Merit Award, Classic Brits & Gramophone Lifetime Achievement Award, and induction into the Hollywood Bowl Hall of Fame. Sir James received an Order of the British Empire (OBE) award in 1979, and Knighthood in 2001 from Queen Elizabeth II.

Editor's Notes

Fantaisie, written in 1912, is dedicated to Leopold Lafleurance, who at the time was solo flutist in the Paris Opera. The beginning, *moderato quasi fantasia* allows you to shine with its free style. The *Assez lent*, is the middle section of the piece and should be played according to the tempo markings suggested by the composer. At bar 41 there is a cadenza leading to the conclusion of part one of the piece. The second part of the *Fantaisie* gives you the opportunity to show off your finger technique and triple tonguing. I would recommend you practice your trills, which will add a nice touch of brilliance to the piece.

Nocturne and Allegro Scherzando was commissioned as a required concours piece for students at the Paris Conservatory in 1906 and dedicated to Philippe Gaubert's teacher and mentor, Paul Taffanel. It is indeed a real test piece for any flutist. The *Nocturne* is an opportunity for you to show off your best tone colors and intonation. The *Allegro Scherzando* is a great test for your fingers and gives you some idea of the standard of the flute class in the Paris Conservatoire. In the middle of all the fireworks, the piece returns to the beginning theme, but in the second octave. It finishes with some very difficult scales, arpeggios, double tonguing and octaves.

Madrigal is one of Gaubert's most performed works. It is considered a great introduction to Gaubert's style. The work begins in the lower register and returns there throughout the piece. Underlying the seemingly simplistic melody is the need for perfect synchronization of the flutist and pianist to execute the parallel harmonies in the piece.

The *Third Sonata* was composed in 1933 for Jean Boulze, solo flutist of the *Opéra et des Concerts Lamoureux*. In the first movement, *Allegretto*, I would recommend that you play with a tempo a little on the quick side. The reason for this is that it helps enormously with the breathing. A light touch upon the keys also helps toward the success of this piece. The key to the second movement also lies in the tempo, *Tres Moderé*. Do not be tempted into playing too slowly but try at all times to play with your most beautiful tone, again using a light touch upon the keys. The third movement should not be too slow in spite of the *Joyeux - Allegretto* tempo suggestion from Gaubert. The sonata is a wonderful piece and is a great opener for any recital.

Breathing and Posture

• Breathing is one of the most important and neglected elements in the quest for a good tone.

• Without a good breath control your chances of having the tone of your dreams will remain a dream.

• In order to obtain a beautiful tone you need to begin with your posture.

• Good posture is essential for good breathing. Without a good posture you cannot attain good breathing.

• I was fortunate as a teenager to learn the flute with a singer. She taught me to have a good posture and with it good breathing. They go hand in hand.

• There are plenty of singing demonstrations on the Internet connected with breathing and posture and I would urge you to look there for help.

• Nearly every book on singing contains a lot of material about posture and breathing. I suggest you look at something like *Singing for Dummies* as a good place to start.

• In my editions for Southern Music I have put in many breath marks, sometimes more than you might think necessary. I don't want to be short of breath at the conclusion of a phrase. One should have enough breath to support the tone at all times. Good breath control is the secret of a great tone.

The breath marks are of two kinds: (√) being a very quick and short breath whereas (') is a regular breath mark. For a short breath, I would recommend that you don't open your mouth so much but that you acquire the technique of taking a lot of breath through your lips in the embouchure position.

Sir James Galway

à L. Lafleurance

Fantaisie
for Flute and Piano

Philippe Gaubert
edited, arranged and performed by
Sir James Galway

Flute

Flute

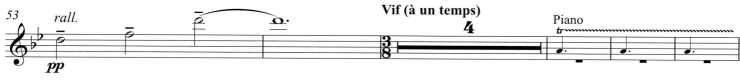

Flute

Flute

à mon cher Maître Paul Taffanel, Professeur au Conservatoire

Nocturne and Allegro Scherzando
Nocturne

Flute

Philippe Gaubert
edited, arranged and performed by
Sir James Galway

Flute
Allegro Scherzando

Flute

Flute

à Docteur Bucquoy
de l'Académie de Medecine

Madrigal
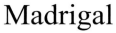

Philippe Gaubert
edited, arranged and performed by
Sir James Galway

Flute

Flute

à Jean Boulze
Flûtiste solo de l'Opéra et des Concerts Lamoureux

Sonata No. 3
for Flute and Piano

Flute

Philippe Gaubert
edited, arranged and performed by
Sir James Galway

I.

Flute

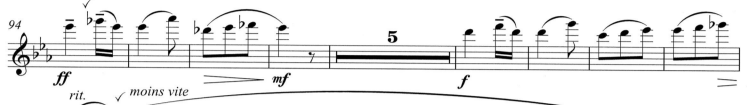

Flute

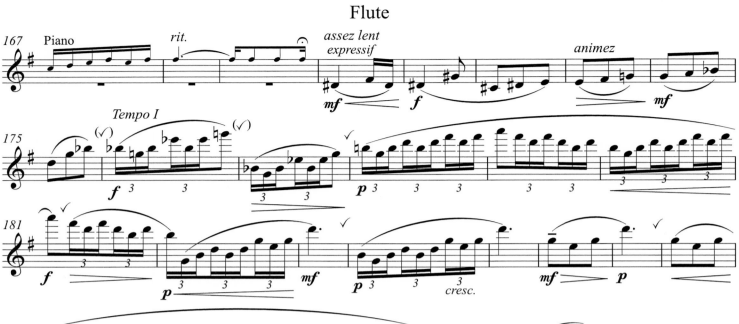

II. Intermède pastoral

Flute

Flute
III. Final

Flute

Flute

Un poco animato

Tempo I

rit.

a tempo

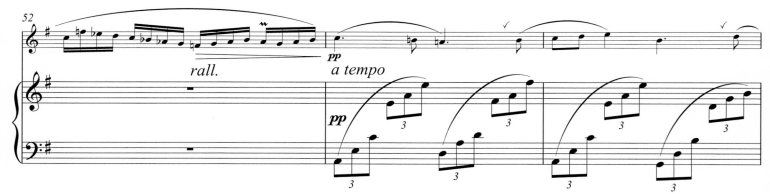

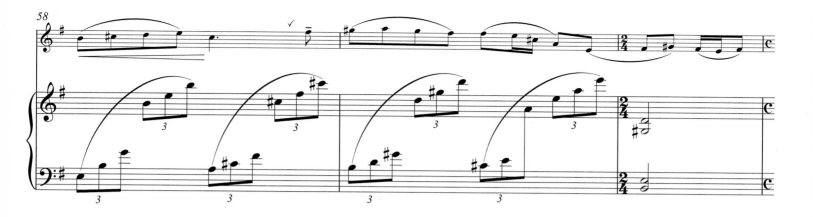

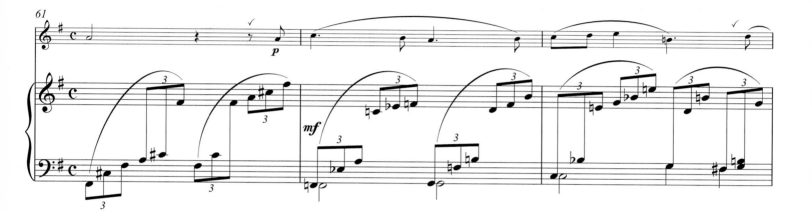

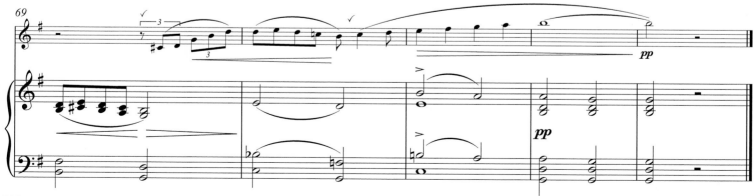

à Jean Boulze
Flûtiste solo de l'Opéra et des Concerts Lamoureux

Sonata No. 3
for Flute and Piano

Philippe Gaubert
edited, arranged and performed by
Sir James Galway

I.

Piano

Flute

Piano

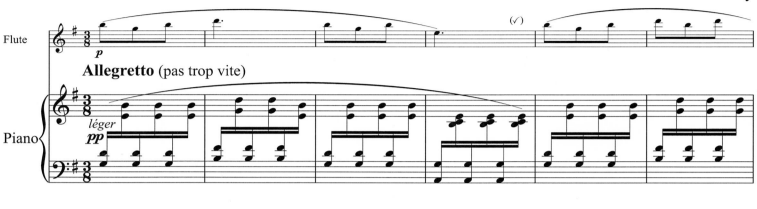

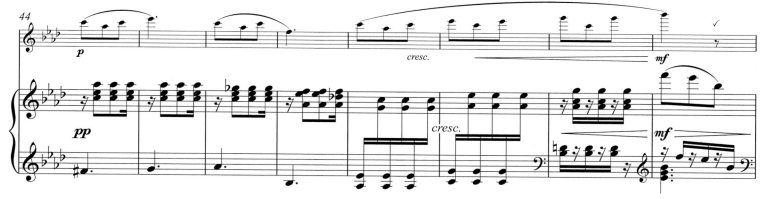

B578

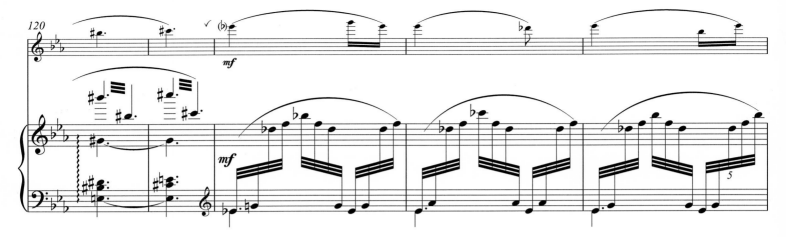

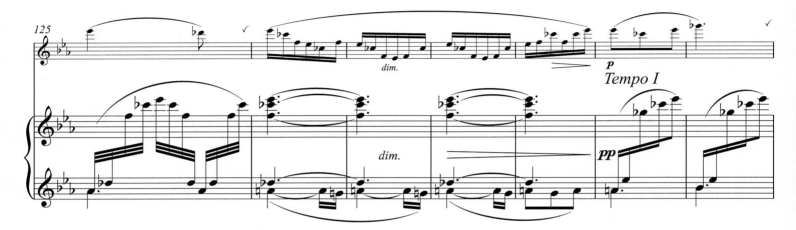

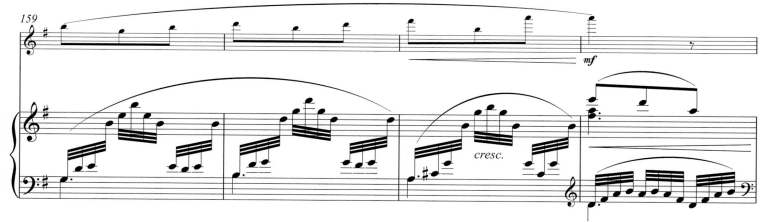

II. Intermède pastoral

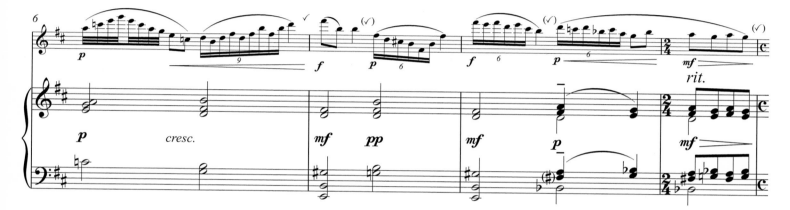

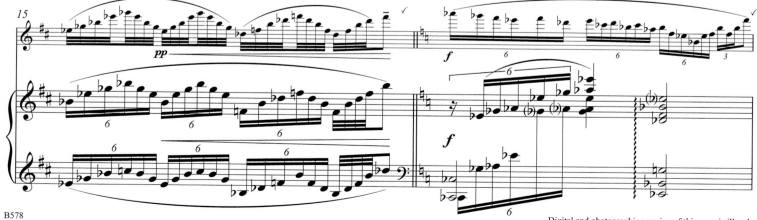

34

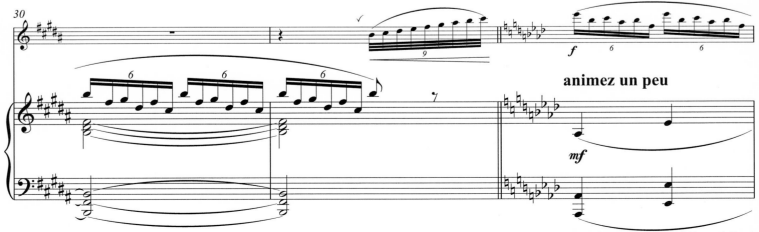

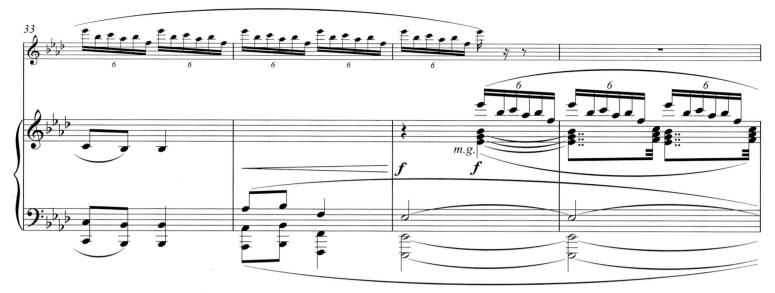

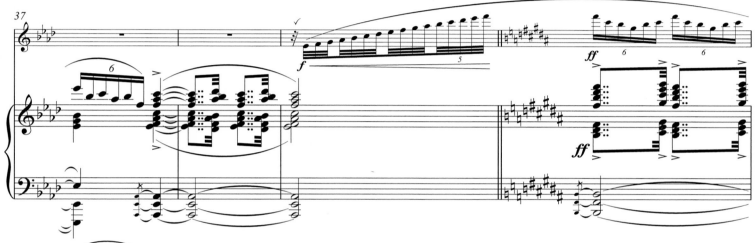

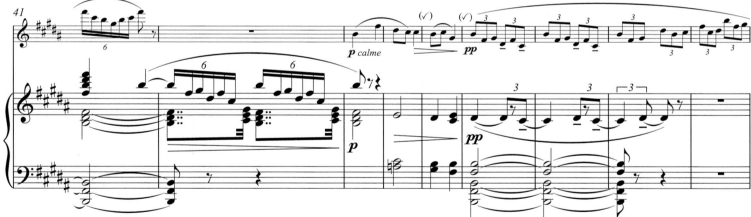

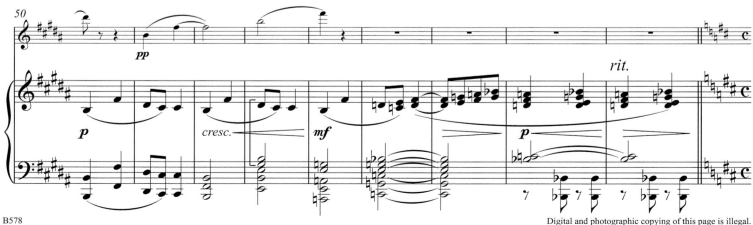

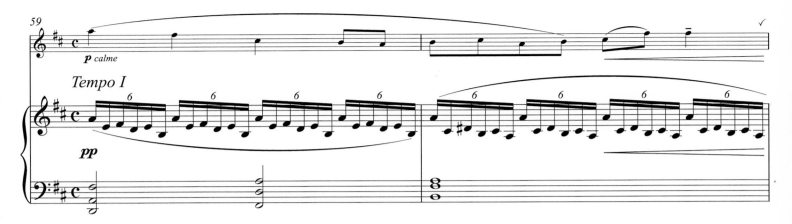

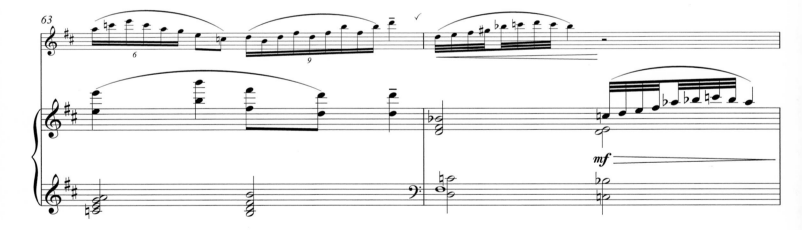

III. Final

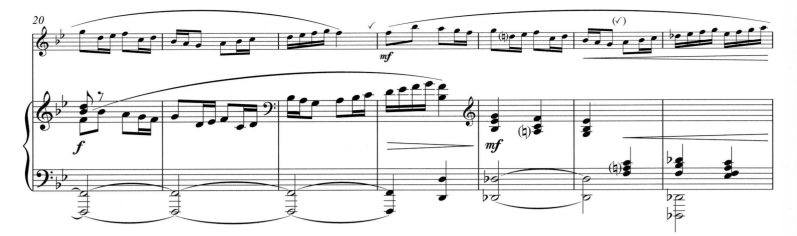

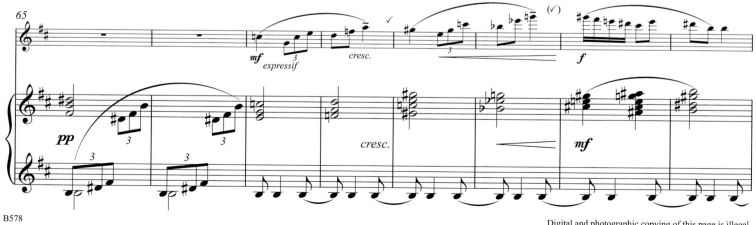

B578

cédez un peu   Tempo I

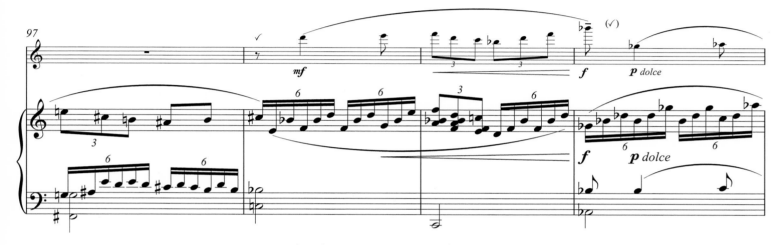

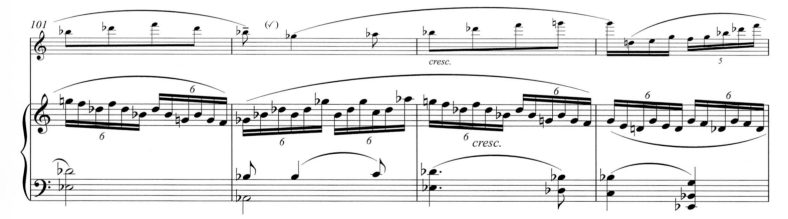

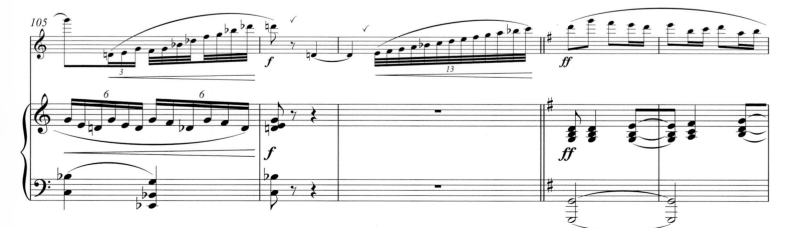

un peu moins vite

expressif

animez un peu

Tempo I

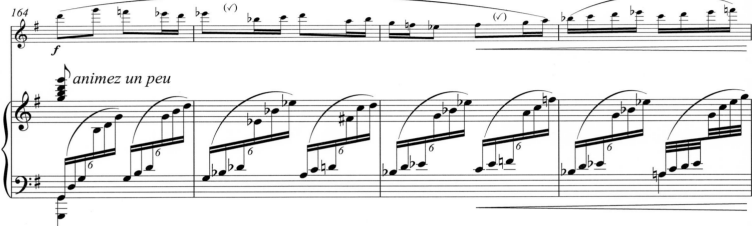